THE FRENCH REVOLUTION AND NAPOLEON

Stephen Pratt

Wayland

Themes in History

Themes in History

The American Frontier
The Crusades
The French Revolution and Napoleon
Life in the Middle Ages
The Rise of Islam
The Roman Empire

Cover illustration: Painting of Lafayette's oath at the
Fête de la Fédération, 14 July 1790.

Opposite: *Sans culottes* sing a patriotic song while dancing around a tree of Liberty.

First published in 1992 by
Wayland (Publishers) Limited
61 Western Road, Hove
East Sussex BN3 1JD, England

Editor: Mike Hirst
Designer: Joyce Chester
Consultant: David Laven, lecturer in history at the University of Keele.

British Library Cataloguing in Publication Data
Pratt, Stephen
The French Revolution and Napoleon.—(Themes
in history)
I. Title II. Series
944.04
ISBN 0 7502 0322 6

Typeset by Dorchester Typesetting Group Ltd
Printed and bound in Italy by
L.E.G.O. S.p.A., Vicenza

Contents

The *Ancien Régime*

In 1774, Louis XVI became King of France. He succeeded his grandfather Louis XV and at the age of twenty, he had become one of the most powerful men in Europe.

Like his grandfather and great-grandfather before him, Louis was an absolute monarch. By law, he had complete power and authority to rule the country exactly as he wanted to. Yet before the end of the century, this system of government was to have been swept away for ever in a bloody revolution. Louis would have lost both his crown and his head, and France would be governed by a man from a much humbler background.

Above *Louis XVI, monarch of the* Ancien Régime, *painted by the artist Duplessis. He is in full ceremonial costume to make him look as grand as possible.*

Right *A contemporary view of the* Ancien Régime: *a bishop and a nobleman, the first and second estates, stand on a peasant, crushed by the weight of his taxes and forced labour.*

French government and society before the Revolution is called the *ancien régime* or old régime. The population was divided into three classes, or estates:

● The First Estate, made up of priests, bishops, monks and nuns who worked in the Catholic Church.
● The Second Estate – the nobility.
● The Third Estate, made up of everyone else, from poor peasants to the rich middle-class townspeople, such as lawyers and merchants, who are often called the bourgeoisie (from *bourg,* an old French word for 'town').

The first two estates had many privileges. Most important, they paid fewer taxes than the members of the Third Estate, even though they were the richest people in France. The great bulk of taxes were paid by the French townspeople and the peasants.

By the middle of the eighteenth century, people from each of these three estates had become discontented with the way France was ruled – though each of the different estates had different reasons for wanting to change the government of their country.

The Hall of Mirrors in the palace at Versailles, just outside Paris. This was the luxurious home of the royal family, and the centre of government of the Ancien Régime.

Watteau was a fashionable painter during the Ancien Régime. *He painted this romantic view of country life for the delight of the court. Compare this view with the harsh realities depicted at the bottom of page 4.*

The peasants were by far the biggest group in French society, and probably the least privileged. Some peasants still lived under the feudal system that remained from the Middle Ages. They farmed land owned by members of the nobility, and every year had to give part of their harvest to their lord. Most of them had to grind their corn at the lord's mill, press their grapes at his wine-press and bake their bread in his oven – all at a price!

Peasants also had to do unpaid work (called the *corvée*) to maintain local roads and bridges. Harsh game laws forbade them to shoot any deer, wild boar or birds, though the nobility could hunt whatever and wherever they liked.

Life was hard for the peasants, but the middle classes who lived in the towns were discontented too. They were very envious of the nobility's privileges. Not only did nobles pay fewer taxes, but all senior jobs in the Army, Navy and the Church were reserved for noblemen. The educated bourgeoisie demanded that careers should be 'open to ability' and not dependent on noble birth.

Even members of the nobility itself criticized Louis XVI's government. They too thought that it was badly run and inefficient. The king's power was supposed to be absolute, but in fact it was often limited. In the provinces, the work of his officers, (called intendants) was often frustrated by local law courts, called *parlements*. The whole legal system was slow and old-fashioned, and the tax collecting system worked badly.

Slowly but surely, Louis XVI's government headed towards bankruptcy. During the eighteenth century France had fought several wars, and, to pay for the army, kings had borrowed large sums of money. The high interest paid on these loans used up much of the government's income. The king, the queen – an Austrian princess called Marie Antoinette – and many of the wealthiest nobles lived lives of reckless luxury in the magnificent Palace of Versailles about 10 kilometres outside Paris. The court used up yet more of the nation's wealth. The government had no annual budget to show how much money it received in taxes and spent each year. So no one even knew the exact state of the country's finances.

Many people felt that they could run the country better, and demanded radical change. In most towns there were literary and debating societies where lively discussions on politics took place. Many books demanding reform were published and widely read. Authors and philosophers such as Voltaire and Jean-Jacques Rousseau wrote books that questioned the traditional ideas about the way people

Jean-Jacques Rousseau, one of the most widely read authors of the Enlightenment. His book, The Social Contract *began, 'Man is born free, and everywhere he is in chains.' His ideas had a powerful influence on the Revolution.*

An illustration from Diderot's Encyclopédie, *depicting a new mechanical cider press. The radical thinkers from the age of the Enlightenment believed human reason was capable of making endless scientific as well as political progress.*

lived. They wanted people to have more tolerant attitudes, and to look at the world more scientifically. Many of their ideas were reflected in the first French encyclopaedia, called *L'encyclopédie*, edited by Denis Diderot in the mid eighteenth century. Historians describe this new kind of thinking as the Enlightenment.

Some French people began to demand a constitution – a set of rules designed to control the way a government works. They also wanted to form an assembly of representatives, elected by the people to draw up laws and give advice to the government.

The problems of Louis XVI's government finally came to a head in the 1780s. The king had staved off bankruptcy by borrowing more and more money, but he was finally unable to borrow any more. The only solution seemed to be a new tax on land, to be paid by the nobility.

Unfortunately for Louis, the *parlement* of Paris, along with all the other main law courts of France, refused to recognize the new tax. Moreover, most of the clergy and nobility decided to back the courts' opposition to the king.

November 1787, the Duke of Orleans publicly opposed the new tax decreed by the king's government, and denounced the exiling of the Parlement *of Paris when they refused to register it.*

Some nobles genuinely wanted a thorough reform of the government. Others supported the *parlements* simply because they resented the king's attack on their privileges. To make their opposition clear, in some regions of France, the nobles and the *parlements* organized riots and even attacks on the king's intendants.

This revolt of the nobility made it almost impossible for Louis to carry on ruling the country as an absolute monarch. He seemed to have only one choice of action: on 8 August, 1788, he called a meeting of the Estates General.

The Estates General was a sort of parliament, made up of elected representatives from the clergy, the nobility and the middle classes. Each of the three estates would meet and debate in three separate chambers. They gathered, at Versailles, in May 1789; it was the first meeting of the Estates General since 1614.

In the 1780s, probably the greatest pressure for reform came from the nobility. Yet the least privileged people in France belonged to the Third Estate, and as the Revolution went on, they would make their voices heard more and more. In January 1789, a priest, the abbé Siéyès, wrote a pamphlet entitled *What is the Third Estate?* This is an extract from it:

What has the Third Estate been up till now? Nothing! It demands to count for something . . . The Assembly of the Third Estate represents 25 million men, and is concerned with the interests of the nation. The [Assemblies of the] other two [estates], even when combined, represent a mere 200,000 individuals, who think of nothing but their privileges.

What kind of people would this pamphlet have appealed to, and what do you think was its appeal?

Abbé Siéyès, the revolutionary pamphleteer. His writings helped create the atmosphere in which the Third Estate turned itself into the National Assembly.

The National Assembly 1789–91

In this painting, The Tennis Court Oath, *the artist of the Revolution Jacques-Louis David tried to make the events of 20 June 1789 look as heroic as possible.*

The meeting of the Estates General at Versailles soon ran into difficulties. The bourgeois deputies from the Third Estate wanted all three estates to meet together and draw up a new constitution. When the king opposed this change, the deputies declared themselves 'The National Assembly of Representatives of the French People'. They were unable to get inside their meeting chamber (probably an accident), so they moved to a nearby indoor tennis court instead. There, they swore an oath to stay together until they had established a new constitution. Soldiers were sent to disperse them, but the deputies stood firm. At last, the king gave in to their demands, and asked the Clergy and Nobility to join them in a new, National Assembly.

Once the National Assembly had been established, many people thought that they had achieved all the reforms that were needed. But, in fact, unrest was on the increase.

Throughout France, food was in short supply, and riots broke out across the country. The National Assembly seemed like the poorer classes' only hope. Meanwhile, Louis XVI, encouraged by his wife, Marie Antoinette, and a group of influential aristocrats, had second thoughts about the reforms he had set in motion. He called troops to Versailles and, on 11 July 1789, dismissed Necker, a popular government minister who claimed to support reform.

Angry demonstrators filled the streets of Paris and revolutionary leaders made violent speeches in cafés and public gardens. Army barracks were looted for weapons. A rumour spread that ammunition was stored in the Bastille, the great royal fortress where enemies of the king were held prisoner without trial. It was attacked on 14 July. The governor was muddle-headed, the mob furious and brave, and the Bastille fell. The king no longer controlled Paris.

The march of the women to Versailles, 5 October 1789. Note that they are followed by the National Guard in their blue uniforms, and are waving the new tricolour, the flag of the Revolution.

The disused monastery of St Jacques which gave its name to the group of determined reformers of the Jacobin Club. Robespierre was a leading Jacobin.

Violence also increased throughout the countryside. Mobs attacked and burnt castles and manor houses. Desperate, hungry peasants destroyed feudal records. On 4 August, amidst great excitement, the National Assembly voted to abolish feudalism.

On the one hand, the middle-class deputies in the National Assembly needed the support of the poor to put pressure on the king. On the other hand, the middle classes were also frightened by the revolutionary violence. In Paris, they formed a new town council and organized an amateur military force in case the revolution should get out of control. Other towns soon followed suit. These military units came to be called The National Guard.

Food shortages and revolutionary disturbances continued into the autumn. On 5 October, a large crowd, mainly of women, marched from Paris to Versailles, demanding bread. They broke into the palace and dragged the royal family off to Paris, where they were kept virtual prisoners in the Tuileries Palace. The National Assembly followed, and Paris now became the seat of government.

Paris was full of excitement. Cafés echoed with violent discussions and the work of the Assembly was hotly debated in new political clubs. Two strong political groups emerged:

● The Jacobins, who took their name from the disused monastery of St Jacques where they met. They were determined middle-class reformers, led by the lawyer Robespierre.

● The Cordeliers, led by the fiery Danton. They spoke for the *sans culottes*, the poorer people in Paris and other large towns. (The name *sans culottes* comes from the fact that poor people wore ordinary trousers and not the culottes, or knee breeches, that were fashionable among the wealthy.)

In the autumn of 1789, the National Assembly set to work. Its main task was to work out a new constitution for France. But as Louis XVI now had virtually no power, the Assembly also had to concern itself with some of the day-to-day government of the country.

The Assembly did away with many of the restrictive laws of the *ancien régime*. All jobs were opened to the Third Estate; Protestants and Jews were now allowed to have French citizenship; the law courts were reformed, and punishments made more humane; torture was abolished. Many trade restrictions were also removed. In particular, customs duties were abolished on goods that were transported from one region of France to another.

The people celebrated when the old customs barriers inside France were abolished, bringing about the freeing of trade. Does it look as though this act of the National Assembly was popular?

One of the National Assembly's first acts was to draw up a *Declaration of the Rights of Man and of the Citizen*. It was meant to be a statement of the basic principles on which the new government of France would be based. The *Declaration* stated:

We want to make a declaration for all men, for all time, for all countries, and which will be an example to the world.

The *Declaration* included the following statements:

● **Men are born and remain equal in rights. Social distinctions can be based only on individual usefulness for the general good.**
● **Property is inviolable and sacred.**
● **The free communication of thought is one of the most precious rights of man.**
● **Freedom from oppression is guaranteed.**

Which of the National Assembly's reforms helped to fulfil the promises of the *Declaration*?

In this painting the Declaration of the Rights of Man is presented very impressively, as though engraved on stone tablets like the Ten Commandments.

An assignat, *which was a sort of credit note. The National Assembly tried to help government finances by confiscating all church lands, selling them, and using the money to support the* assignats.

One of the Assembly's most important acts was to reform the Church, the First Estate. All Church land was confiscated and sold. The money was used to pay for the government and guarantee the paper money that it issued. The Church itself was reorganized by the 'Civil Constitution of the Clergy'; bishops and priests were to be elected, paid by the government and made to swear an oath of loyalty. This Civil Constitution split the French Church in two, between those priests who accepted it and swore the oath, and those who refused, called the non-jurors (or non-swearers).

Yet the Assembly was beset by problems. Unrest continued in both Paris and the countryside, and spread even to the armed forces. There were also fears that plots were being hatched by 'enemies of the Revolution' – non-jurors, *émigrés* (aristocrats who had fled abroad) and even the king. Suspicions against the king increased in June 1791, when the royal family tried to escape from Paris to the north-east frontier of France. They travelled in disguise for twenty-four hours, but were recognized at the village of Varennes and sent back to Paris.

The king's flight was a major problem for the National Assembly. It was about to suggest that France should become a constitutional monarchy. Under the new constitution, the king would be head of state, governing with the help of a parliament elected by the middle classes. Yet, by trying to leave the country, Louis had hardly shown any support for such a constitution.

The deputies and their supporters now split. Moderate deputies restored the king and made him swear an oath to the new constitution. Republicans wanted to do away with the king altogether, and replace him with an elected council. The Jacobins were divided, the Cordeliers firmly republican. On 14 July 1791, Paris was thronged with crowds celebrating the second anniversary of the fall of the Bastille. Three days later, a huge republican demonstration took place in the city. At the Champ de Mars, a large open space in the west of Paris, the republican supporters gathered to draw up a petition demanding the abdication of the king. Frightened by this display of republican feeling, the Mayor of Paris declared martial law and the National Guard turned out. Shots were fired, the demonstration became a riot and fifty republicans were killed.

The Revolution was sliding further towards violence, civil war and terror.

A medal issued during the constitutional monarchy. The motto, 'Live Free or Die', encircles the words 'The Nation, the Law, the King'. Why was all this too optimistic?

A popular contemporary picture of the humiliating arrest of Louis XVI and his family at Varennes, 22 June 1791.

The Fall of the Monarchy 1791–3

In spite of the growing cries for a republic, it was a constitutional monarchy that was set up. According to the rules of the new constitution, a new parliament, called the Legislative Assembly, was elected by middle-class voters in October 1791.

A strong group within the new Assembly were the Brissotins, supporters of a politician named Brissot. He launched strong attacks on the king and enemies of the Revolution. He also began to urge that Revolutionary France should go to war against the old regimes in other parts of Europe – especially Austria and Prussia.

Above *Jacques Pierre Brissot, leader of a group of middle-class deputies known first as Brissotins and then Girondins. They became bitter enemies of the more extreme Jacobins.*

Right *This savage cartoon shows the revolutionaries' hostility to the aristocratic emigrés, who are depicted as desperate, helpless old men, aided and abetted by a hypocritical priest on the right of the picture.*

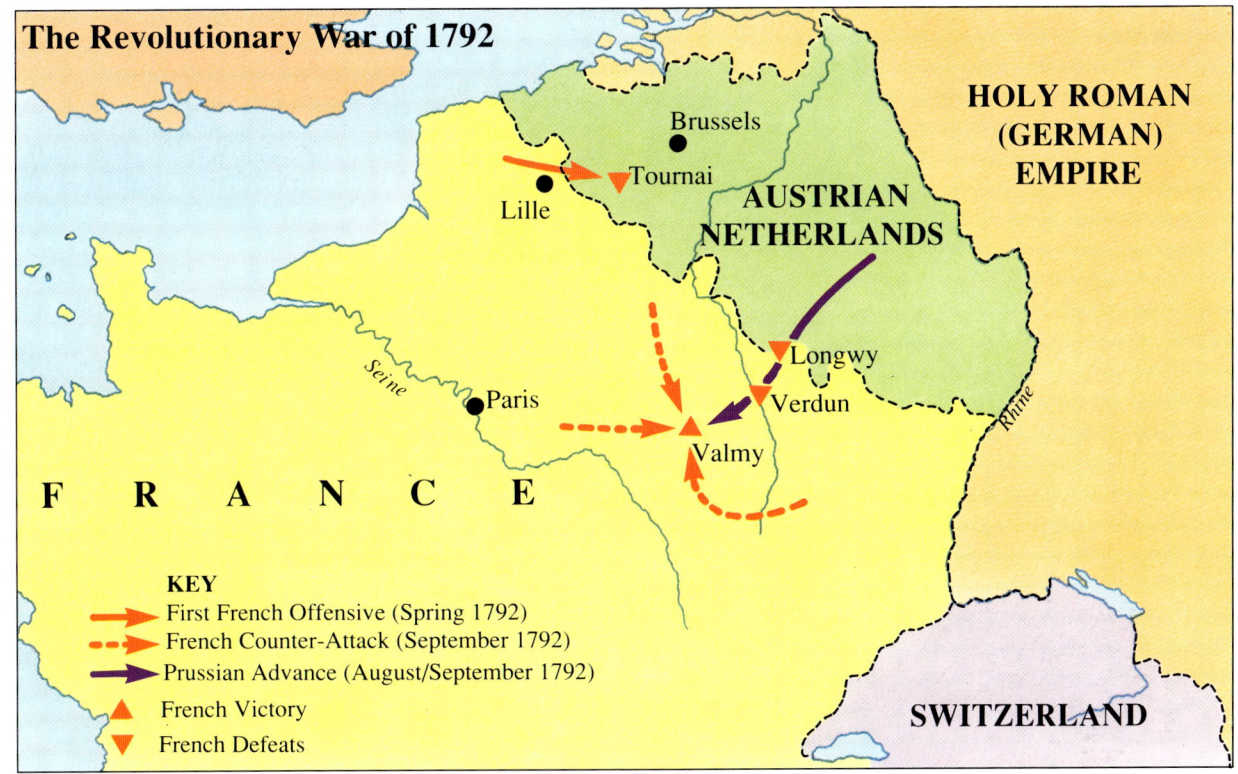

The Revolutionary War of 1792

KEY
First French Offensive (Spring 1792)
French Counter-Attack (September 1792)
Prussian Advance (August/September 1792)
French Victory
French Defeats

This map shows the areas of confrontation during the 1792 war.

There were two reasons for fighting the Austrians and Prussians.

● First, the Brissotins wanted to spread the Revolution and help France's neighbours, particularly in Germany and the Austrian Netherlands (now Belgium), to win freedom from their aristocratic rulers. 'War on castles, peace to cottages', was the Revolutionary cry.

● Second, many French people feared that the Austrians were plotting with aristocratic *emigrés* and the Catholic Church to launch a counter-revolution and restore the absolute monarchy.

War was declared against Austria and Prussia in April 1792, with almost complete support in the Legislative Assembly. Unfortunately, the deputies had paid little attention to the condition of the French Army. It was in a dreadful state – small and badly-equipped. Many of the aristocratic officers had emigrated and whole regiments split up. Not surprisingly, as soon as the Army tried to advance over the frontier it was disastrously defeated. The road to Paris was now open to the Prussian Army.

The song of the fédérés of Marseilles. It achieved such popularity that it became the main song of the Revolution, and ultimately the French national anthem.

Treachery was also suspected, and, in fact, Marie Antoinette had sent the French plan of campaign to the Austrians in March. The Assembly passed new laws against non-jurors and *émigrés*, and summoned extra groups of the National Guard, called *fédérés*, to Paris. The king tried to veto, or refuse, these laws, but the *fédérés* marched to Paris nevertheless. Those from Marseilles sang a new revolutionary song which became the French national anthem: the *Marseillaise.*

As the Prussian Army advanced, the people of Paris became more and more excited. On 20 June 1792, a mob broke into the Tuileries Palace and terrified the royal family. Screaming 'Down with the veto!', they forced Louis to drink a toast to the Nation.

The Brissotins now began to regret the troubles that they had unleashed, and decided that they would actually like to protect the constitutional monarchy. But more extreme Jacobins, headed by Robespierre, were already plotting with the *sans culottes* leaders and the *fédérés* against the king. They formed a Revolutionary Committee at the Paris Town Hall and planned an attack on the Tuileries Palace.

On 10 August 1792, an armed mob again attacked the Tuileries. The royal family fled to the Legislative Assembly, leaving the king's guard to protect the palace. It was captured by the mob after a ferocious battle in which around 1,200 people were killed.

The royal family was imprisoned, and the constitutional monarchy abolished. The victorious Revolutionary Committee declared itself the new Commune, or town council, of Paris. The Legislative Assembly was dismissed, and replaced by a new Convention, to be elected by all adult males. A Revolutionary Tribunal was set up to deal speedily with people suspected of being enemies of the Revolution. Many royalists, nobles and non-jurors were arrested, tried quickly and sent to the guillotine. This new machine for beheading criminals was a popular spectacle.

Paris itself was still threatened by the advancing Prussian Army, and in a state of increasing panic. Patriotic feeling was whipped up by Danton's rousing speeches: 'We must be daring, still more daring, even more daring', he said, 'and Paris will be saved.' Thousands of young men flocked to join the Army and build the defences of Paris. But the panic also led to more mob violence. Between 2 and 7 September, armed gangs invaded the Paris prisons and massacred at least 1,100 prisoners. Only a third of these were political suspects; the rest were ordinary criminals.

This picture celebrates the patriotism aroused in Paris by fear of the advancing Prussians, and Danton's speeches. Volunteers flocked to enrol in the army.

A contemporary picture of Louis XVI and his family being taken to the Temple prison.

In fact, the panic that Paris might be attacked turned out to have been unjustified. On 20 September, the Revolutionary Army stopped the Prussian advance at the Battle of Valmy. The Prussian general retreated, and France was safe.

When the new Convention met, it contained two rival groups. The Brissotins were still powerful, and had received much support in the provinces, particularly in the Gironde area of south-west France. (From now on, the Brissotins were often also called the 'Girondins'.) But they were challenged by the more radical Jacobins, working closely with the Paris Commune and the *sans culottes*. Robespierre pressed for the king to be executed for treason. The Brissotins were unable to save him, and in January 1793, Louis was beheaded.

Throughout the spring of 1793, the Jacobins grew in power, until, in June, they once again used the Paris mob to attack their enemies. A huge crowd surrounded the Convention, and twenty-nine Brissotin deputies were arrested.

9 Louis XVI's valet stayed with the king until he was taken away for execution. He later wrote:

I remained alone in the room, numb with grief. The drums and trumpets announced that His Majesty had left the prison. An hour later, salvoes of artillery and cries of *Vive la Nation!* and *Vive la République!* filled the air. The best of kings was no more.

Why do you think the king's death caused different people to react in such different ways?

PROCLAMATION
DU
CONSEIL EXÉCUTIF
PROVISOIRE.

EXTRAIT des Regiftres du Confeil, du 20 Janvier 1793, l'an fecond de la République.

Above *The proclamation by the provisional council of the death sentence passed on Louis on 21 January 1793.*

Left *An artist's impression of the execution of Louis XVI. The executioner holds up the king's head for the crowd to see.*

Along with Marie Antoinette, they were sent to the guillotine in October.

The Jacobins now ruled France. The Convention continued to exist, but the real government was now a Committee of Public Safety, a group of twelve men led by Robespierre. For the next year, they were to rule ruthlessly.

21

The Committee of Public Safety 1793–4

Maximilien Robespierre, a dominant member of the Jacobin Club, and ruthless leader of the Committee of Public Safety, and government by Terror.

The Committee of Public Safety found itself at the head of an unstable, disunited nation. Many areas of the country had rebelled against the government in Paris. In Lyons, the National Guard revolted against the Jacobin council, and there was a Girondin uprising in the Vendée region of western France.

The Committee acted ruthlessly against its opponents, both in the provinces and in Paris itself. With the help of the Revolutionary Tribunal, the Jacobins imprisoned anyone who was suspected of opposing them. Many of these suspects were sent to the guillotine. The rebellions in the provinces were put down in a savage civil war. It has been estimated that 3,000 people were executed in Paris, and a further 14,000 in the provinces. This period, from June 1793 until July 1794 is know as the Terror. Few people were safe from the fear of arrest.

Robespierre believed that the Terror was needed to give France strong revolutionary government. Under his leadership, the Committee of Public Safety appointed *représentants en mission*, or government agents. They went into the provinces to make sure that the Committee's decrees were carried out. The aristocracy had been abolished and French

Revolutionary playing cards. Kings, Queens and Knaves have been replaced by patriotic citizens.

France 1793-4

UNITED PROVINCES (THE NETHERLANDS)

HOLY ROMAN (GERMAN) EMPIRE

ENGLISH CHANNEL

AUSTRIAN NETHERLANDS

Arras

Le Havre

Rouen

Caen

Rheims

Metz

Seine

Paris

Nancy

Brest

Rhine

Rennes

Orleans

Angers

Nantes

Dijon

Loire

F R A N C E

SWITZERLAND

BAY OF BISCAY

Lyons

Rhône

Bordeaux

PIEDMONT

Gironde

Orange

Marseilles

Toulon

KEY

Area of Vendee uprising

Centres of counter-revolution and execution during the Terror

SPAIN

people were now told to call each other *citoyen* (citizen) instead of *monsieur* or *madame*. A new revolutionary calendar was introduced. Year I of the Republic began on 22 September 1792, and twelve new months were invented with poetic names such as *Brumaire* (foggy), *Ventôse* (windy), *Germinal* (budding) and *Thermidor* (hot).

France in 1793–4 was unstable and disunited. All over the country people tried to rebel against the government, but were crushed.

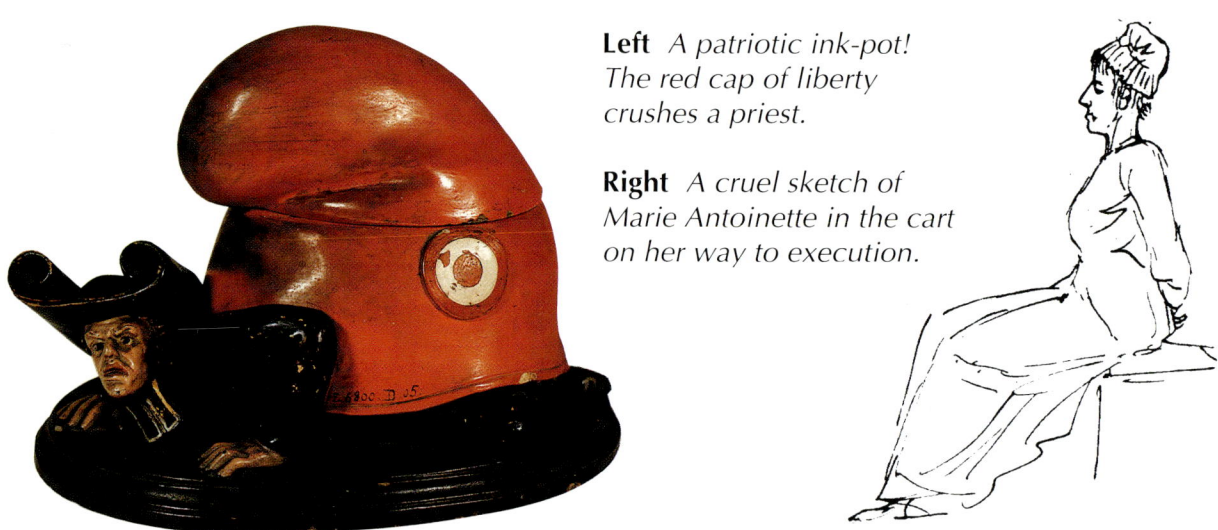

Left *A patriotic ink-pot!
The red cap of liberty
crushes a priest.*

Right *A cruel sketch of
Marie Antoinette in the cart
on her way to execution.*

Below *Under the
Committee of Public Safety
France was better prepared
for war and successfully
annexed territory in the
east.*

More and more, the government opposed the Catholic
Church. In Paris, churches were closed or turned into Temples of Reason. Robespierre himself wanted to introduce a
Republic of Virtue and a new republican religion worshipping the *Etre Suprême* or Supreme Being.

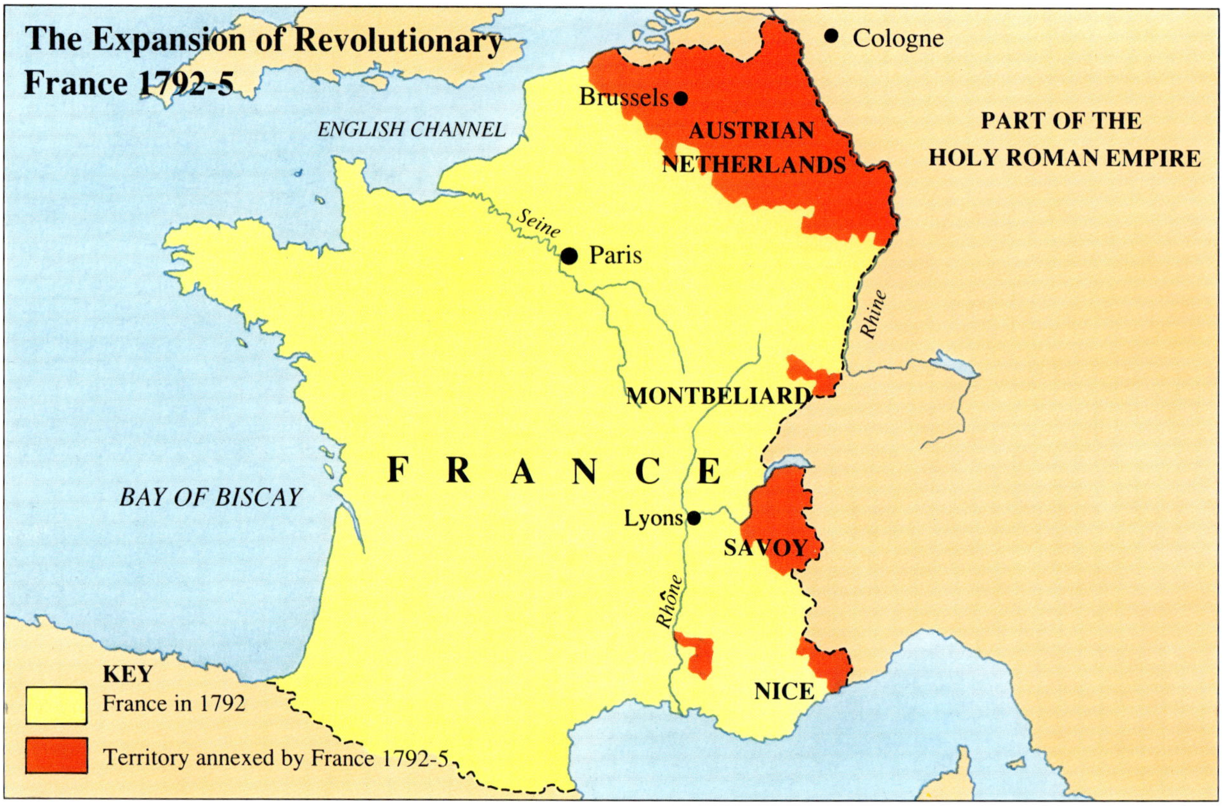

**The Expansion of Revolutionary
France 1792-5**

ENGLISH CHANNEL

Cologne

Brussels

AUSTRIAN
NETHERLANDS

PART OF THE
HOLY ROMAN EMPIRE

Seine

Paris

Rhine

MONTBELIARD

BAY OF BISCAY

F R A N C E

Lyons

SAVOY

Rhône

NICE

KEY

France in 1792

Territory annexed by France 1792-5

Under the Committee of Public Safety, France also renewed its wars against the enemies of the Revolution abroad. The enemies now included not only Prussia and Austria, but also England and Spain. This time, however, France was better prepared for war. The government had introduced conscription – forcing all young men to join the army. They were led by new, younger generals. The Committee also organized the manufacture of weapons.

The Revolutionary Armies were now successful. The Austrians were pushed out of the east of France, and in June 1794 France reoccupied the Austrian Netherlands.

In spite of France's military successes, food shortages and price rises continued. In the spring of 1794, unruly mobs of *enragés*, or angry people, once again demonstrated on the streets of Paris. Yet the Jacobins, who had so often used the Paris mob, now clamped down on it. In March, the leaders of the *enragés* were executed. The Terror increased.

The Committee of Public Safety tried to draw the whole of France into the war effort. For the first time in the country's history, everyone was supposed to do something to support the army. This decree was issued in 1793:

All French people are in a state of permanent mobilization for the service of the armies. The young men shall go to battle; the married men shall forge arms and transport supplies; women shall make tents and serve in hospitals; the children shall tear bandages; and old men shall go to public squares and preach the unity of the Republic and hatred of kings.

However, many people in France resented the conscription and high taxes that were demanded by the Revolutionary Government in Paris. How might people in the provinces have reacted to this decree?

This poster emphasized the indivisible unity of the Republic and proclaimed, 'Liberty, Equality, Fraternity or Death.'

More propaganda. The patriotic citizen who wears 'Liberty' on his hat, 'Equality' on his coat, 'Fraternity' on his dagger, and 'or death' on his pistol. Patriots were expected to fight fiercely against enemies of the Revolution.

Gradually, even radical politicians and members of the Committee of Public Safety themselves began to dread the Revolutionary Tribunal. In April 1794, Danton, who had criticized Robespierre, was sent to the guillotine, and between April and July a further 2,356 people were executed. Who would be next?

Afraid for their lives, a group within the Committee of Public Safety plotted against Robespierre. On 26 July, he went to the Convention and made a speech against his enemies, but when he tried to speak again the following day, there were cries of, 'Down with the tyrant!' Robespierre's colleagues called for his arrest. His old supporters – the *sans culottes*, the Paris Commune and the Revolutionary Tribunal – failed to rescue him. On 10 Thermidor (August), Robespierre and seventy-one of his followers were executed.

¶ During the Reign of Terror, St Just, a friend of Robespierre, wrote:

Between the people and their enemies there can be nothing in common but the sword, we must govern by iron those who cannot be governed by justice, we must oppress the tyrant. It is impossible for revolutionary laws to be executed unless the government itself is truly revolutionary.

However, other people saw the Terror in a very different light. Madame Roland was the wife of a leading Girondin who was sent to the guillotine. She wrote:

We have made mistakes . . . The pure men whose ardour sought freedom . . . believed that to overthrow despotism would start the rule of justice and peace; but in fact it only heralded a surge of passions most repellent, and vices most hideous.

Why might some people have opposed the Terror and some not?

The Rise of Napoleon 1794–9

The Reign of Terror was over. The Paris Commune was disbanded and the Jacobin club closed. The Revolutionary Tribunal, which had sent so many people to the guillotine, was also abolished. Many leaders of the *sans culottes* had been executed on Robespierre's orders, and the Paris mob, which had played such an important part in the Revolution, quickly lost its influence on French politics.

The middle classes now took firm control of the government. There were two new assemblies, with elected deputies, but in fact between 1794 and 1799 the real government rested with a group of five men called the Directory.

Under the Directory, life in Paris changed drastically. Free from the strict controls of the Committee of Public Safety, the middle classes now indulged in extravagant displays of wealth. Instead of the humble *sans culottes*, the streets of Paris were full of rich young people, dressed in fancy, fashionable clothes.

Above *Burning* assignats *in Paris in 1796. After the fall of the Committee of Public Safety,* assignats *became absolutely worthless. The Directory was faced with high inflation and valueless paper money.*

Left *A romantic depiction of Napoleon leading a heroic charge across the bridge at the victory of Arcole. The political views of the artist are obvious!*

Some people felt that France was returning to the old ways of the *ancien régime* – marked by both poor government and the extravagant living of the wealthy. A report into public finance observed that: 'There is no branch of public life which has not been penetrated by corruption and immorality . . . salons are reviving the immoral customs of the preceding era.'

Abroad, the French Army continued its conquests. Its career system allowed able young officers to rise quickly in the ranks and become generals. One of these was a young Corsican, Napoleon Bonaparte. In 1796–7 he invaded and conquered northern Italy. New 'sister republics' were formed and the *ancien régime* overthrown – though the French conquerors also took vast sums of money and works of art from northern Italy. Other generals carried out the same policy in Switzerland, Rome and Naples.

Italy in 1798.

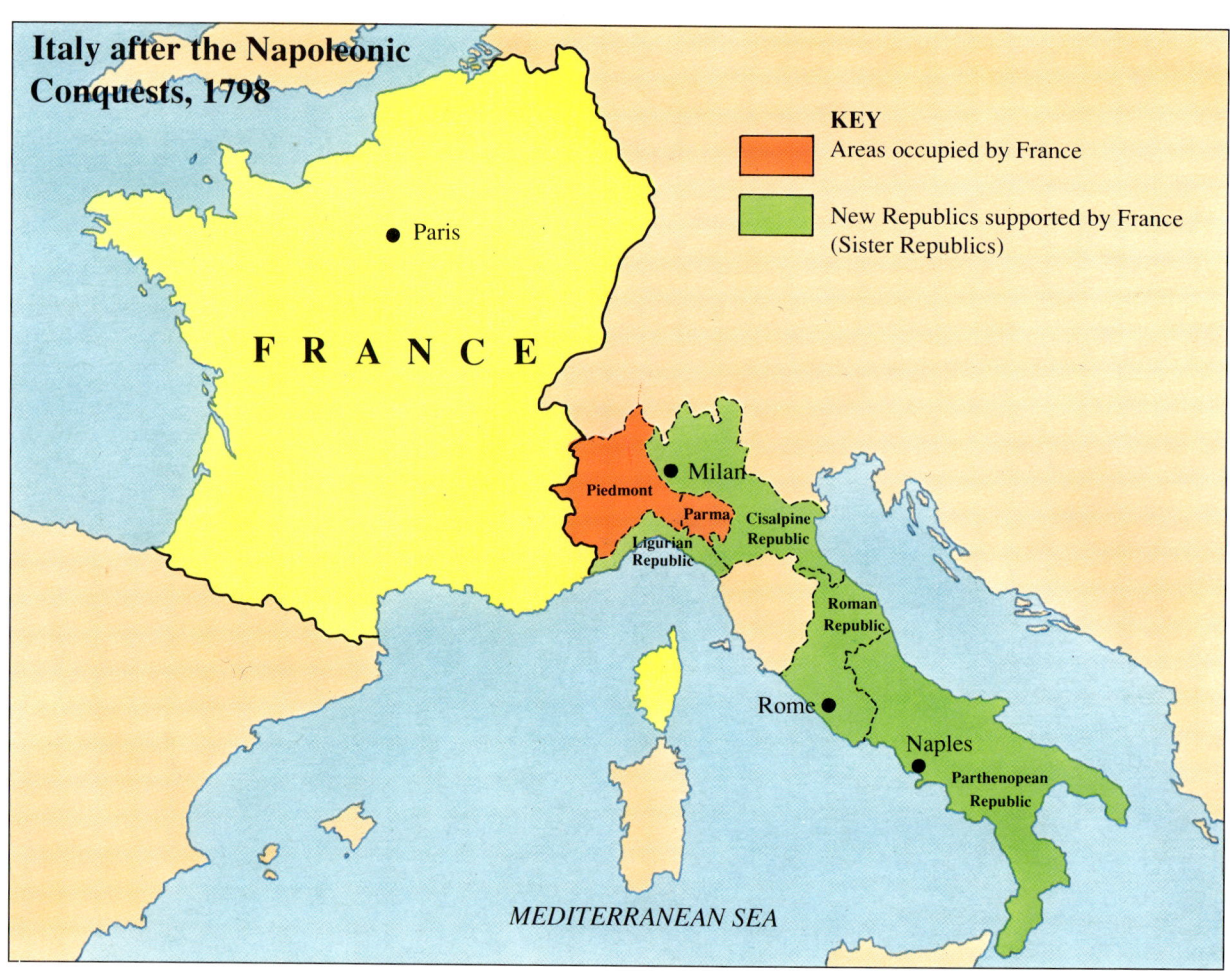

Italy after the Napoleonic Conquests, 1798

KEY

Areas occupied by France

New Republics supported by France (Sister Republics)

Paris

FRANCE

Piedmont

Milan

Parma

Cisalpine Republic

Ligurian Republic

Roman Republic

Rome

Naples

Parthenopean Republic

MEDITERRANEAN SEA

The army also began to interfere more and more in French politics. The Directory never dealt successfully with the serious problems of the food supply, inflation and law and order. It was attacked by both royalists (who wanted to restore the monarchy with Louis XVI's *émigré* brother as king) and Jacobins. There were serious riots, and the Directory was saved only because the Army protected it. Napoleon in particular had close links with one of the Directors, Paul Barras.

Napoleon was ambitious, and the Directory's weakness played into the hands of the general's political ambitions. In 1799, he plotted with his supporters and one of the Directors, and on 9 November (or 18 *Brumaire*) Bonaparte's troops dismissed the Directors and elected deputies. A new government of three consuls was declared, with Napoleon as First Consul. Within a year, the constitution was twisted to give him supreme power.

The First Consul now announced: 'Citizens, the Revolution is established on the principles with which it began. It is complete.' The middle classes, dazzled by Bonaparte's military success, and anxious for stability and security, accepted his rule.

In 1798 Napoleon invaded Egypt, but his fleet was destroyed by Nelson at Aboukir Bay, and the French advance into Syria was held up at St John of Acre by British forces. This cartoon shows him leaving Egypt secretly and deserting his army. In spite of this he remained a popular hero.

6

Napoleonic France

Above *A portrait of the young Napoleon as First Consul, painted by Ingres. Napoleon posed for very few portraits.*

The First Consul quickly set about reorganizing the government of France. After the Revolution, the country had been divided up into forty-seven departments (or counties). Napoleon decreed that each department should be controlled by a prefect. Departments were themselves divided into *arrondissements*, under sub-prefects, and each town or commune had a mayor. All these local officers were appointed by Bonaparte, and through them he controlled every corner of France.

Gaudin, a clever financier from the *ancien régime*, was made minister of finance. With the new, efficient government, it became possible to collect taxes properly for the first time in many years.

Bonaparte also realized that in order to achieve national unity, he needed to heal the religious divisions in France. He signed a Concordat, or agreement, with Pope Pius VII in 1802. Roman Catholicism was now recognized as the religion of most French people. In return, the government would be allowed to appoint bishops and would pay the salaries of priests.

Right *A* Te Deum *was sung in the cathedral of Notre Dame to celebrate the Concordat between France and the Pope. This reconciliation between France and the Catholic Church was an important part of Napoleon's policy of creating national unity.*

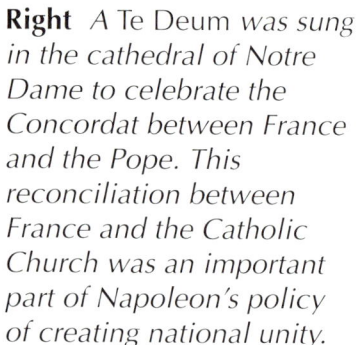

Napoleon governed with the help of a Council of State, which contained men from many different backgrounds – ex-Jacobins, ex-royalists and moderates. Led energetically by the First Consul, the Council produced a new code of civil law in 1804. This system of laws, which became known as the Code Napoleon, replaced the confused system of many different laws that had existed before and during the Revolution.

As First Consul, Napoleon appeared at his best: a young (he was barely thirty), vigorous leader, listening seriously to the advice of the ablest men he could find. France had unity, security and stability after years of upheaval. Yet Napoleon's rule also had its drawbacks, and the First Consul seemed to have almost unlimited ambition.

France continued to defeat its enemies in Europe until peace was declared in 1802. Napoleon now used a great wave of popularity and public support to make himself First Consul for the whole of his life (instead of for just ten years).

The Arc de Triomphe in Paris. Napoleon's architects drew their ideas from the great buildings of ancient Rome. They designed buildings in a grand style, to celebrate the Emperor's great victories.

Louis David, who was first the artist of the Revolution, then of the Empire, painted this spectacular picture of the coronation of Napoleon in Notre Dame. It is a good example of the Empire style which sought to make everything appear as grand as possible.

Then, in 1804, it was announced that: 'The government of the Republic is entrusted to a hereditary Emperor.' Napoleon became emperor, with the right to pass on the title to his children after his death.

Napoleon and his wife, Josephine, were crowned at a spectacular ceremony in the Cathedral of Notre Dame in Paris. The emperor and empress moved into the Tuileries Palace, and a whole new aristocracy was created. Napoleon believed that 'mankind is governed by baubles', and he created a Legion of Honour to reward good service. He also created new princes, dukes, counts and barons, whose titles were supported by grants of land, usually in the countries France had conquered.

Napoleon was also determined to stamp out any opposition to him. In 1800, he suppressed sixty out of seventy-three newpapers in Paris. By 1811, strict censorship had reduced the number to four. A new ministry of police imprisoned opponents without trial, and Jacobins suspected of plotting against the emperor were locked up or executed. In 1809, Napoleon created the University of France, really a government department to control all schools and make sure that loyalty to the emperor was taught at all levels.

Under the Empire, the elegance and delicacy of the eighteenth-century furniture and decoration was replaced by stiff, ornate settees and chairs, lavishly decorated with gold and ormolu (gilded bronze), befitting the heroes of a great military empire.

The Emperor also dismissed some of his best ministers and replaced them with loyal supporters who never disagreed with him. He was determined to keep all power in his own hands.

In 1810, Napoleon divorced Josephine because she had not given him an heir. Instead, he married Marie Louise, the daughter of the Emperor of Austria. Some French people were shocked that the man who had led the Revolutionary, republican armies to victory should now join himself to one of Europe's most powerful royal families.

Napoleon has always been a controversial figure in French history. These three passages were written by three of his advisors. What do they tell us about Napoleon? How did the three advisors differ in their attitude towards the Emperor?

● I still regarded Napoleon as the unique necessary man, as our sole guarantee against the recurrence of a revolution . . . but I did not shut my eyes to his faults, or to his misuse of power, or to the baneful effects of his flatterers. (Duc de Broglie)

● In the years of the Consulate he held several councils every day. There all questions of administration, finance and jurisdiction were debated. He would often throw in profound comments, judicious reflections which astonished those who had most experience in these matters. (Jean Antoine Chaptal Conte de Chanteloup)

● The more I saw of him, the more firmly I was persuaded that, always under the sway of the moment, he thought of nothing but of magnifying himself and his power. (Count Mole)

Napoleon's European Empire

By 1802, France controlled Belgium, Holland, most of northern Italy and Switzerland. Spain became Napoleon's ally. France's only neighbour to remain completely independent was Britain.

Britain was the main threat to Napoleon. It organized coalitions of other European nations against France, and supplied these allies with large sums of money. Unlike other European countries, Britain could not be defeated by a land army, so Napoleon worked out a mighty invasion plan.

One hundred thousand men and 2,000 ships were gathered near Boulogne, ready to invade Britain. The French and Spanish Navies then tried to lure the British Navy out of the English Channel, so that the invasion fleet could cross in

This print was published in France in 1803, showing how England might be invaded by air, sea and land. The hot-air balloon had been invented in the eighteenth century, but the Channel tunnel had to wait 190 years!

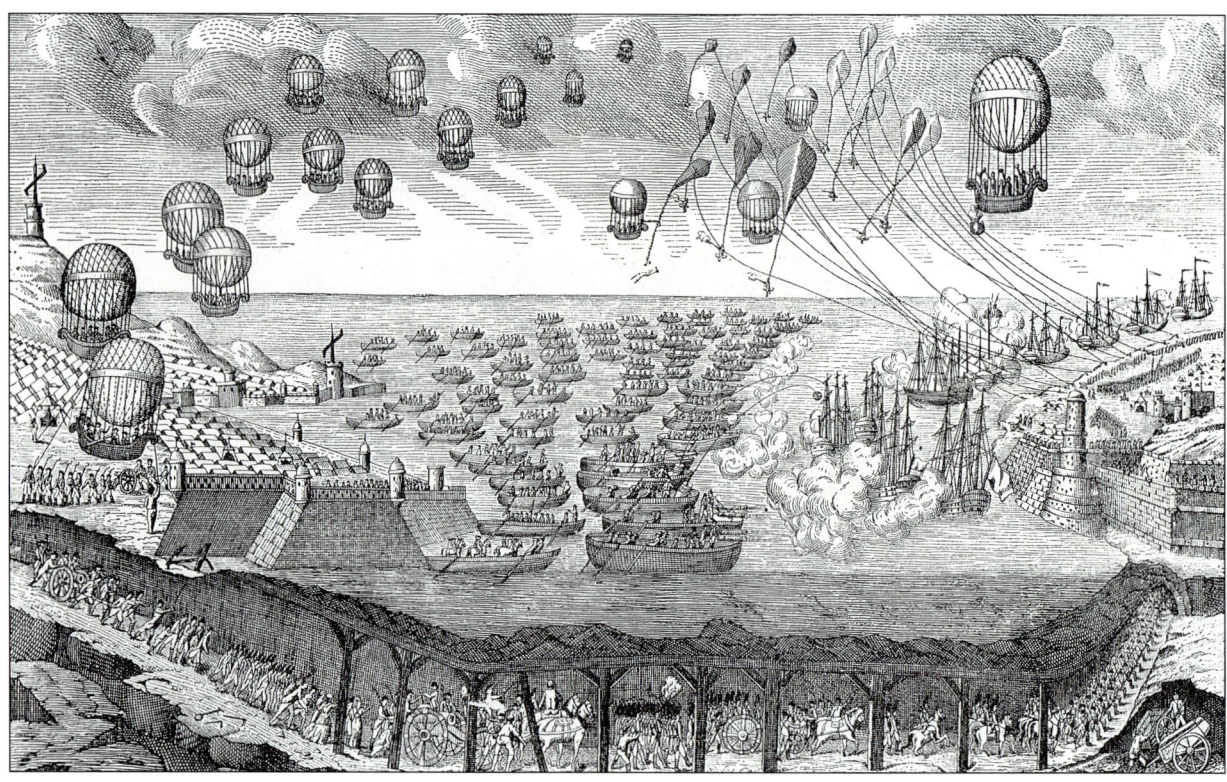

safety. However, in October 1805, the British Navy, led by Admiral Nelson, fought and destroyed the Spanish and French fleets at Trafalgar in southern Spain, and Napoleon had to abandon his invasion plans.

Although the British remained supreme at sea, their allies were not so successful on land. Napoleon moved his troops from Boulogne into central Europe, where they defeated the armies of Russia and Austria at the Battle of Austerlitz. The Russians retreated and the Austrians made a humiliating peace with the French. Napoleon then invaded and occupied Prussia, crushing the Prussian Army at the Battles of Jena and Auerstädt in 1806. After two further battles against the Russians (at Eylau and Friedland), the Russian tsar also made peace with the French.

By the end of 1807 Napoleon's European Empire had already almost reached its height. In Germany, sixteen of the largest states were organized into the Confederation of the Rhine, closely linked to France. The Emperor also

Europe at the height of Napoleon's power, 1812.

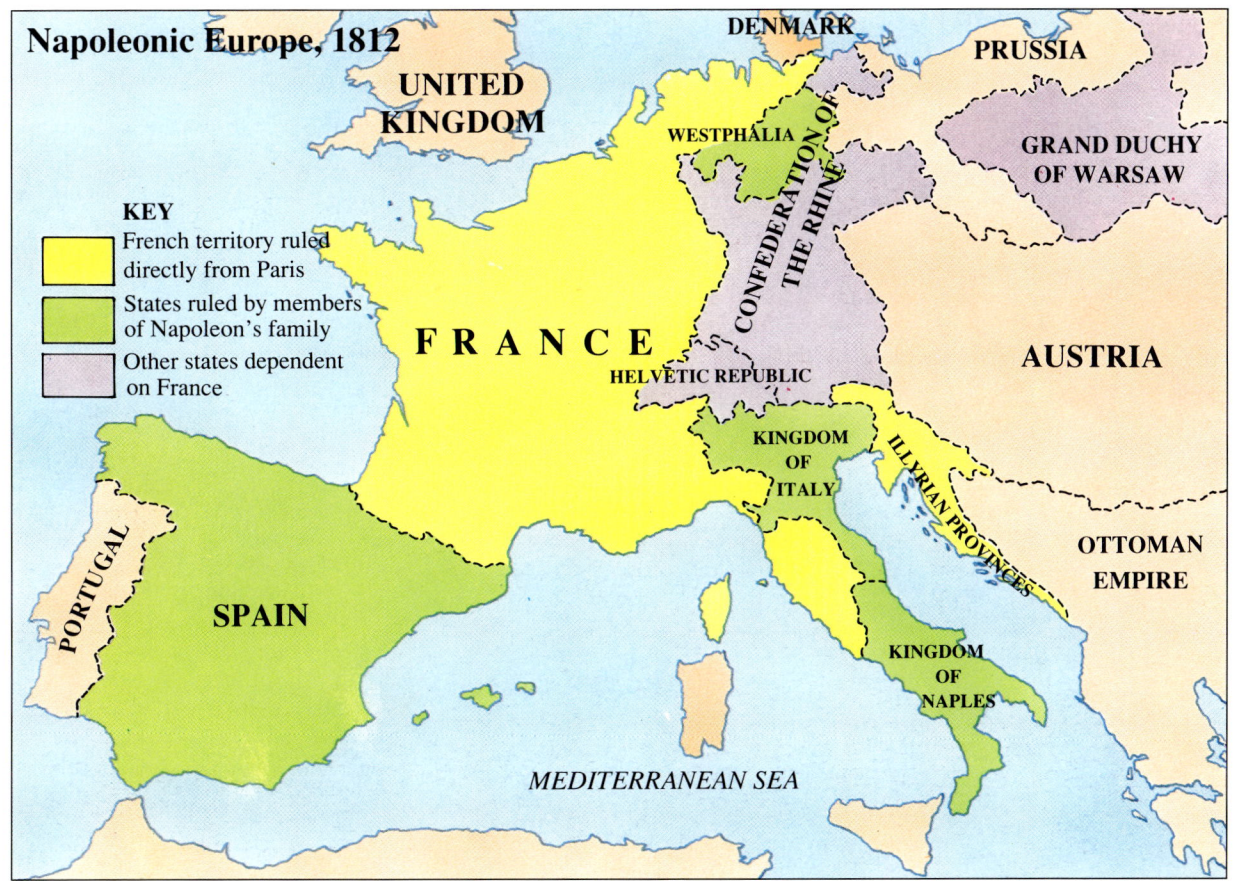

Napoleonic Europe, 1812

KEY
- French territory ruled directly from Paris
- States ruled by members of Napoleon's family
- Other states dependent on France

UNITED KINGDOM
DENMARK
PRUSSIA
WESTPHALIA
CONFEDERATION OF THE RHINE
GRAND DUCHY OF WARSAW
FRANCE
HELVETIC REPUBLIC
AUSTRIA
KINGDOM OF ITALY
ILLYRIAN PROVINCES
OTTOMAN EMPIRE
PORTUGAL
SPAIN
KINGDOM OF NAPLES
MEDITERRANEAN SEA

After defeating Prussia and then Russia 1806–7, Napoleon made peace with Tsar Alexander I on a raft anchored in the middle of the River Nieman, at Tilsit in 1807. This contemporary Viennese picture shows Napoleon with Alexander on his right and Frederick William III of Prussia on his left.

placed his generals and members of his family at the head of conquered states. In Germany, Jerome Bonaparte became king of Westphalia and Marshal Murat was made Grand Duke of Berg. Joseph Bonaparte became king of Naples, Louis Bonaparte king of Holland. Northern Italy was ruled by a viceroy, Napoleon's stepson. In fact, every state in the empire was a disguised dictatorship. Whether it was ruled by one of Napoleon's brothers, a general or a local ruler who submitted to France, Napoleon controlled them all.

Although Napoleon was not a democratic ruler, he did introduce many of the reforms of the French Revolution throughout the Empire. Feudalism was abolished and the privileges of the old nobility swept away. The Code Napoleon, the Concordat and French methods of taxation were imposed everywhere. In many countries the middle classes welcomed these aspects of Napoleon's government, just as the French Third Estate had welcomed the sweeping away of the *ancien régime* in 1789. However, there were also drawbacks to French rule. The conscription and the high taxation that Napoleon imposed weighed heavily on the people in the countries that the French conquered.

Malta, bone of contention. This English cartoon from 1803 shows the English defying Napoleon's claims to Malta. Anglo-French rivalry continued even during the short-lived Peace of Amiens, March 1802 – May 1803.

Britain remained the one thorn in Napoleon's side. For as long as it remained independent, there was a chance that the British would try to fund another coalition of European powers against France. Napoleon argued that Britain's wealth came from seaborne trade, and that if this trade were destroyed, the British would have to submit to French control of Europe.

Ever since 1793, French governments had forbidden the import of British goods. In 1803, Napoleon extended this ban to the ports all along the North Sea coast in Holland and Germany. After occupying Prussia in 1806, he issued the Berlin Decrees: no trade with Britain was allowed in any part of the French Empire. Any goods from Britain or its colonies would be seized. As part of Russia's peace agreement with France, the tsar also agreed to close all Russian ports to British goods. This blockade of trade was known as the Continental System.

The Continental System did indeed damage British trade, though Britain found many different ways of fighting back against the blockade: neutral ships were made to carry British licences, or risk being seized by the British Navy; British goods were smuggled into the French Empire, or entered via the Papal States (the part of Italy around Rome), Spain and Portugal – countries that were, in theory, neutral. Britain also exported goods to South America and the USA.

Napoleon tried desperately to make the Continental System work. He occupied the Papal States, and made the Pope a prisoner. In 1808, a French Army marched across Spain to occupy Portugal, and then the Spanish king himself was replaced by one of Napoleon's brothers.

However, Napoleon's struggle to enforce the Continental System aroused opposition to him from within the French Empire. In Spain, local committees of priests and nobles, called *juntas*, raised a rebellion against the foreign king and his French Army. In Portugal, the French Army was actually defeated by a British Expeditionary Force.

Napoleon believed that the middle classes of Europe would welcome French rule and the new political ideas that came from France. In 1807, he wrote to his brother, King Jerome of Westphalia:

In Germany as in France, Italy and Spain, people long for equality and liberalism. The benefits of the Code Napoleon, legal procedure in open court, these are the points by which your monarchy must be distinguished.

Yet the Continental System and the endless wars had very negative effects on Napoleon's Empire. The Comte de Segur wrote:

The success of the Continental System depended on how long Napoleon could control a subject and suffering Europe, deprived of all colonial goods or paying excessively high prices for them, facing the collapse of all maritime trade and the restriction of all trade by land. How was it possible to impose these changes, this burden, this ruin on so many people?

How might you have felt if you had been a merchant in Germany at this time?

The effects of the Continental System. French soldiers search the baggage of a German citizen to check if he has any English goods.

Encouraged by this news, anti-French feelings began to stir in Germany and Austria, and in 1809, Austria once again declared war on France. Napoleon rushed across Europe from Spain, and after a hard-fought campaign, finally defeated the Austrians at the Battle of Wagram. Once again, the Austrian Emperor made peace with the French.

Meanwhile, the effects of the Continental System became worse and worse. The French Army tried to clamp down on smuggling in Holland and Germany, and all British goods were seized and burnt. Sugar, cotton and other goods imported from outside Europe were in short supply and very expensive. Throughout Europe, merchants suffered from the effects of Napoleon's trade blockade.

The renewed fighting also took a heavy toll. To pay for his wars, Napoleon imposed heavier and heavier taxation, and young men were conscripted from all over the Empire, to fight wherever Napoleon chose. Throughout Europe, people began to object to the high price of Napoleonic government.

Napoleon at the battle of Wagram, 1809. Another picture designed to glorify the Emperor as a great military conqueror.

Napoleon's Fall and His Legacy

General Frost shaving little Boney. This English cartoon from 1812 caricatures Napoleon, who has just suffered the defeat and retreat from Moscow through the snows of a Russian winter.

From 1809 onwards, the French position in Spain got worse and worse; Napoleon himself complained of what he called the 'Spanish ulcer'. The British Army occupied Portugal, where the commander, later to become the Duke of Wellington, spent three years building up his forces. In Spain, French forces were continually troubled by bands of guerrilla soldiers who attacked outposts, stores and roads. Then, in 1812, the British advanced into Spain and inflicted a crushing defeat on the French.

France's relationship with Russia also suffered problems. Napoleon had wanted to marry a Russian princess, but the tsar refused to allow such a move. The Russian nobility despised Napoleon as an upstart, and Russian merchants bitterly resented the damage to their trade from the Continental System. In 1810, the tsar reopened his ports to British trade, and Napoleon decided that another war against Russia was necessary.

Napoleon advanced into Russia in June 1812, with 450,000 men, conscripted from all over the Empire, in a Grand Army. The Russians retreated, burning their towns and crops. This 'scorched earth' policy meant that the French could not replenish their supplies as they advanced deeper and deeper into Russia. At Borodino, the two armies finally met in a desperate battle, at which Napoleon lost 30,000 men. Two weeks later he entered Moscow, only to find the city on fire and all the Russian officials fled.

After five weeks, Napoleon had to order the retreat from Moscow across barren land. His troops were repeatedly attacked by Russian forces and soon floundered in the snow of the Russian winter. Thousands starved or froze to death. Of the Grand Army, only 40,000 men managed to struggle home to France.

The Russian campaign sounded the death knell for Napoleon's Empire. The Russians advanced into Germany and were soon joined by Austria, Prussia and Britain in a

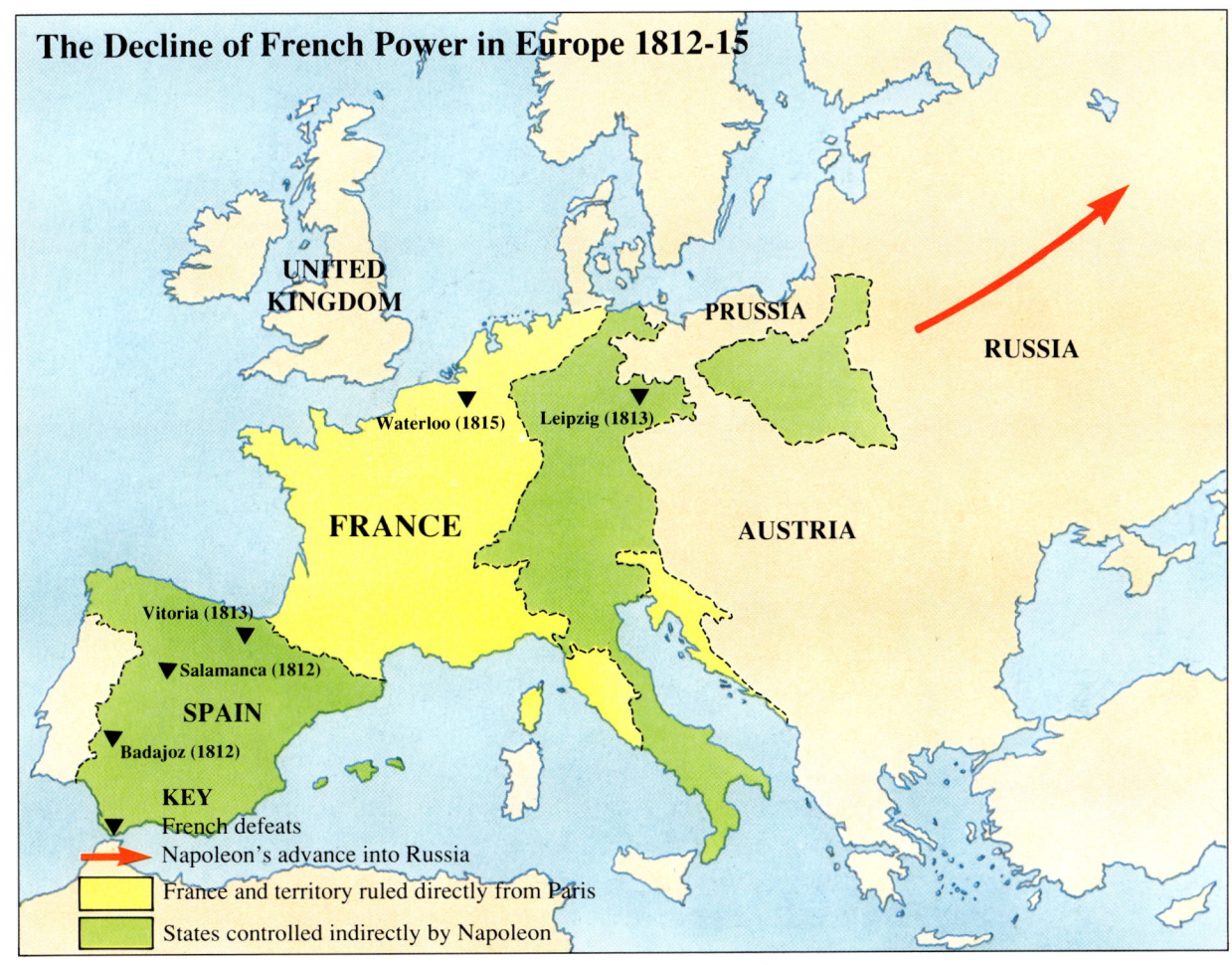

The Decline of French Power in Europe 1812-15

UNITED KINGDOM

PRUSSIA

RUSSIA

Waterloo (1815)   Leipzig (1813)

FRANCE

AUSTRIA

Vitoria (1813)

Salamanca (1812)

SPAIN

Badajoz (1812)

KEY

▼ French defeats

→ Napoleon's advance into Russia

France and territory ruled directly from Paris

States controlled indirectly by Napoleon

fourth coalition against France. Napoleon managed to raise 150,000 troops and met the allies at Leipzig in 1813, but after three days of bitter fighting, he was defeated and retreated, having lost 60,000 men. Then, in June 1813, came the news that Wellington had defeated the French in Spain and ended the French occupation.

When the allies invaded France, the country was exhausted and war-weary. Paris surrendered and the marshals withdrew their support for Napoleon. He abdicated, and a treaty with the allies made him ruler of Elba, a tiny island off the coast of Italy.

However, Napoleon still had a lot of support within France, and the allies found it difficult to impose a new government on the country. In particular, there was bad feeling between the returned *émigré* nobles and the officers of Napoleon's Army.

Napoleon's invasion of Russia in 1812 ended in disaster. His empire collapsed, and Napoleon abdicated.

Napoleon is shown receiving a hero's welcome from French soldiers on his return from Elba. Another artist seeks to glorify Napoleon, his political message is clear.

A jubilant British poster celebrating the defeat of Napoleon and the allied armies' entry into Paris in 1814.

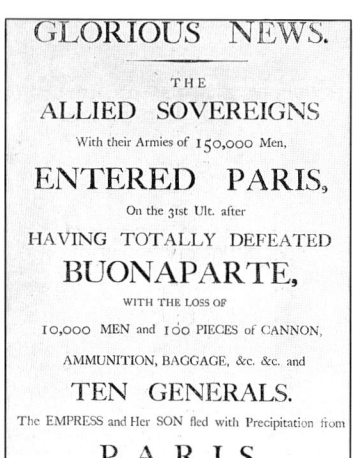

Napoleon soon resolved to act. In Elba, he raised a small army and in March 1815 escaped to the south of France with a thousand men. From there, he marched northward, gathering troops as he went. At Grenoble, the garrison welcomed him with cries of, 'Long live the Emperor!' and by 20 March, Napoleon had reached Paris and was reinstalled triumphantly at the Tuileries Palace.

With his usual speed, on 15 June, Napoleon launched 120,000 men against Wellington and the Prussian general Blücher. At first he outmanoevred the allies, but on 18 June, they met at Waterloo, in Belgium, and the French were defeated. Exactly one hundred days after landing in France, Napoleon was sent as a prisoner to St Helena, a tiny, remote island in the South Atlantic. He died there in 1821.

With Napoleon's banishment to St Helena, the French Empire had finally been quashed. The victorious allies now tried to rebuild Europe, restoring the old rulers wherever they could. Yet would Europeans still be able to live as they had under the *ancien régime*?

The monarchy was restored to France, with Louis XVI's younger brother becoming King Louis XVIII. (There was no Louis XVII as a mark of respect to Louis XVI's son, who had died soon after his father.) Yet Louis XVIII ruled carefully and with a moderate constitution. He kept Napoleon's civil code, his system of local government and education system.

The privileges of the nobility were not restored. When Louis' successor, Charles X, ignored the constitution and tried to rule as a despot, he was overthrown by another revolution in 1830. Charles was replaced by a more liberal constitution and a more liberal monarch, Louis Philippe, nicknamed the 'citizen king'.

Above *The Battle of Waterloo. A lively impression of the battle by a contemporary artist.*

Left *The desolate island of St. Helena.*

Liberty leading the people. The great romantic artist Delacroix painted this dramatic picture to celebrate the revolution of July 1830, and to show that the spirit and ideas of 1789 lived on into the nineteenth century.

Elsewhere in Europe, in Spain, Italy and in many German states, the restored rulers tried to bring back the *ancien régime* and rule without parliaments. They restored aristocratic privileges and kept strict control over the press. Yet, although the people of Europe had suffered under Napoleon – from conscription, heavy taxation and the Continental System – under the French they had also had a taste of what life could be like after the abolition of the oppressive and restrictive *ancien régime*.

The Declaration of the Rights of Man and the French constitution of 1791 remained in the memories of Europe's middle classes long after 1815. So too did the patriotism of Germans, Spanish and Italians who had been ruled by Napoleon. Liberal and nationalistic movements developed and demanded an end to despotism. They wanted new constitutions that would give the middle classes the vote, and ensure the freedom of the press.

Europe had a flurry of liberal revolutions in 1820, 1830 and 1848. Many of them were repressed, but, gradually, the liberals' aims were achieved. The ideals of the years 1789–1815 lived on, and influenced not only the French, but also other European nations, such as Spain, Germany and Italy. In many ways, the whole of modern Europe was born out of the French Revolution and the Napoleonic era.

Timeline

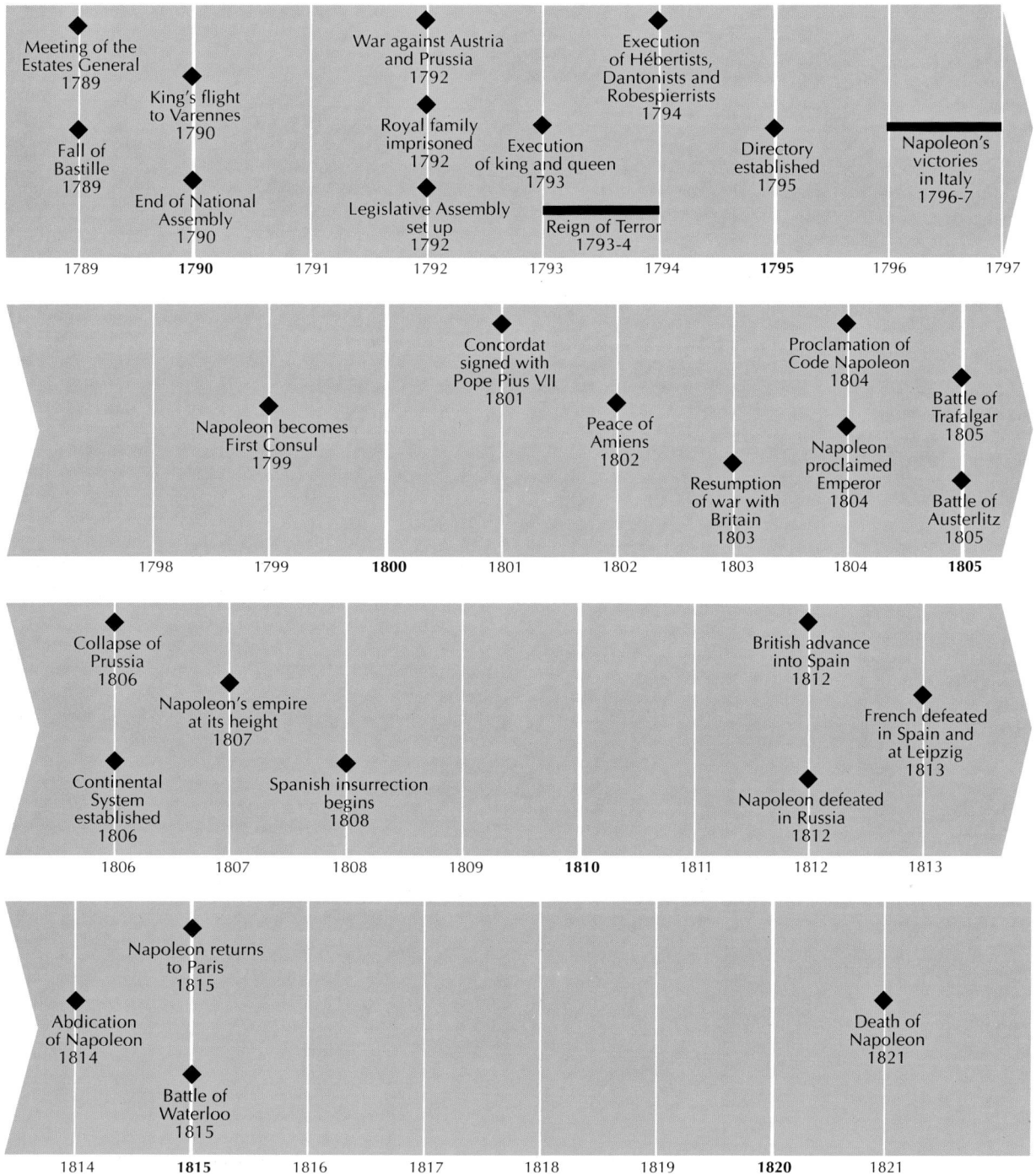

Meeting of the
Estates General
1789

King's flight
to Varennes
1790

Fall of
Bastille
1789

End of National
Assembly
1790

War against Austria
and Prussia
1792

Royal family
imprisoned
1792

Execution
of king and queen
1793

Legislative Assembly
set up
1792

Execution
of Hébertists,
Dantonists and
Robespierrists
1794

Directory
established
1795

Reign of Terror
1793-4

Napoleon's
victories
in Italy
1796-7

1789 **1790** 1791 1792 1793 1794 **1795** 1796 1797

Napoleon becomes
First Consul
1799

Concordat
signed with
Pope Pius VII
1801

Peace of
Amiens
1802

Resumption
of war with
Britain
1803

Proclamation of
Code Napoleon
1804

Napoleon
proclaimed
Emperor
1804

Battle of
Trafalgar
1805

Battle of
Austerlitz
1805

1798 1799 **1800** 1801 1802 1803 1804 **1805**

Collapse of
Prussia
1806

Napoleon's empire
at its height
1807

Continental
System
established
1806

Spanish insurrection
begins
1808

British advance
into Spain
1812

French defeated
in Spain and
at Leipzig
1813

Napoleon defeated
in Russia
1812

1806 1807 1808 1809 **1810** 1811 1812 1813

Napoleon returns
to Paris
1815

Abdication
of Napoleon
1814

Battle of
Waterloo
1815

Death of
Napoleon
1821

1814 **1815** 1816 1817 1818 1819 **1820** 1821

Glossary

Absolute monarch   A king or queen who has absolute power to rule their country as they see fit.

Ancien régime   The name given to the old social and political system of France before the Revolution.

Bourgeoisie   A name for the middle class. (The word literally means 'burgher' or 'citizen'.)

Brissotins   Supporters of the politician Brissot, who first opposed, but later supported the constitutional monarchy.

Code Napoleon   The new system of laws introduced by Napoleon in 1804.

Committee of Public Safety   The group of twelve men who ruled France ruthlessly from 1793 to 1794.

Concordat   Napoleon's pact with the Catholic Church, made in 1801.

Constitution   A set of rules and regulations to control the powers of a government.

Constitutional monarchy   A system of government in which the powers of a king or queen are limited by parliament and the constitution.

Continental System   Napoleon's plan to prevent Britain from having any trade with the rest of Europe.

Convention   The parliament of Revolutionary France from 1792 to 1794. All Frenchmen were allowed to vote in the elections for the Convention.

Cordeliers   A group of radical politicians who received support from the poor of Paris.

Corvée   Unpaid work that some French peasants were forced to do.

Emigrés   Nobles who left France during the Revolution.

Enlightenment   A movement in eighteenth-century philosophy that stressed the importance of science and reason.

Enragés   The unruly mobs of 'angry people' who demonstrated in Paris during the last months of the Committee of Public Safety's rule.

Estates General   The old French parliament that had fallen into disuse in 1614. It met for the very last time at the start of the Revolution in 1789.

Fédérés   Groups of soldiers from the National Guard, summoned to defend Paris in the summer of 1792.

Feudal system   A system of distributing land that was common in Europe during the Middle Ages. Under the feudal system, the lives of the peasants were closely controlled by the nobility.

Girondins   Moderate deputies to the Convention (1792–4), who came from the Gironde region of south-west France.

Intendant   The governor of a French province, appointed by the king.

Jacobins   A group of radical politicians who first met at the disused monastery of St Jacques. They gradually became more and more powerful as the Revolution went on.

Juntas   Committees formed in Spain to organize guerrilla warfare against the French, 1808–12.

Legislative Assembly   The parliament of Revolutionary France from 1791 to 1792. It was elected mainly by the middle classes.

National Assembly The parliament of Revolutionary France between 1789 and 1791.

National Guard The force of volunteer soldiers in Revolutionary France.

Parlements The high courts of France before the Revolution.

Sans culottes The poor people of Paris and other towns, who took part in the Revolutionary disturbances.

The Terror The name given to the period (1793–4) when France was ruled ruthlessly by the Committee of Public Safety, and many 'enemies of the Revolution' were executed.

Books to Read

Olivier Blanc, *Last Letters, Prisons and Prisoners of the French Revolution*, Andre Deutsch, 1987

Josh Brooman, *The Age of Revolution*, Longman, 1992

Charles Dickens, *A Tale of Two Cities*

Nathaniel Harris, *Napoleon*, Batsford, 1988

Christopher Hibbert, *The French Revolution*, Allen Lane,1980

Ken Hills, *French Revolution*, Cherrytree Books, 1988

Picture acknowledgements

Bridgeman Art Library 4 (top), 6, 10, 14 (top), 20, 44; Mary Evans Picture Library cover, 7 (both), 9, 12, 22 (both), 27 (bottom), 30 (bottom), 33, 36, 38, 43 (top); Sonia Halliday 3, 24 (top left); Michael Holford 29; The Mansell Collection 4 (bottom), 11, 14 (bottom), 15 (bottom), 18, 34, 42 (top); Peter Newark 5, 21 (both), 24 (top right), 26, 32, 37, 39, 40, 43 (bottom); Wayland Picture Library 8, 13, 15 (top), 16 (both), 19, 25, 27 (top), 30 (top), 42 (bottom); Zefa 31. Artwork is by Peter Bull.

Index